EARTH AND SPACE SCIENCE

NATURAL HAZARDS

By Christina Earley

A Stingray Book

SEAHORSE PUBLISHING

Teaching Tips for Caregivers and Teachers:

This Hi-Lo book features high-interest subject matter that will appeal to all readers in intermediate and middle school grades. It may be enjoyed by students reading at or above grade level as well as by those who are looking for age-appropriate themes matched with a less challenging reading level. Hi-Lo books are ideal for ELL readers, too.

Each book appeals to a striving reader's age and maturity level. Opportunities are provided for students to read words they already know while encountering a limited number of new, high-interest vocabulary words. With these supports in place, students will read more fluently while increasing reading comprehension. Use the following suggestions to help students grow as readers.

- Encourage the student to read independently at home.
- Encourage the student to practice reading aloud.
- Encourage activities that require reading.
- Establish a regular reading time.
- Have the student write questions about what they read.

Teaching Tips for Teachers:

Before Reading

- Ask, "What do I know about this topic?"
- Ask, "What do I want to learn about this topic?"

During Reading

- Ask, "What is the author trying to teach me?"
- Ask, "How is this like something I already know?"

After Reading

- Discuss how the text features (headings, index, etc.) help with understanding the topic.
- Ask, "What interesting or fun fact did you learn?"

TABLE OF CONTENTS

NATURAL HAZARDS

A natural **hazard** is the threat of a major event in nature that will be harmful.

A natural hazard turns into a natural **disaster** when the threat becomes a real event that impacts humans and the environment.

Scientists classify natural hazards as geological, hydrological, and meteorological.

Some events, like **tsunamis**, fit in more than one category.

FUN FACTS

Climate change is making natural disasters stronger and more frequent.

GEOLOGICAL HAZARDS

Geological hazards are related to changes in Earth's outer layer, or crust.

Earthquakes cause the ground to shake. They can topple buildings and create landslides.

Landslides send large amounts of soil, rock, and other materials quickly down a mountainside.

Erupting volcanoes blast lava, gases, and hot rocks.

HYDROLOGICAL HAZARDS

Hydrological hazards involve water.

Floods come from heavy rainstorms and melting snow and ice.

Storm surge is an unusual rise in water levels due to a powerful storm like a **hurricane**.

Movement of the sea floor can create giant waves called tsunamis. A tsunami can destroy buildings and flood coastlines.

FUN FACTS

The Central China Floods of 1931 were the deadliest natural disaster in world history.

METEOROLOGICAL HAZARDS

Meteorological hazards are threats caused by changes in Earth's **atmosphere**.

A blizzard is a snowstorm with wind speeds of more than 35 miles (56 kilometers) per hour.

Heat waves can cause power outages and crop failures.

When little or no rain falls for a long time, **droughts** dry up soil and make it unable to support plant life.

FUN FACTS

Satellites monitor weather patterns to assist with predicting severe weather, such as hurricanes.

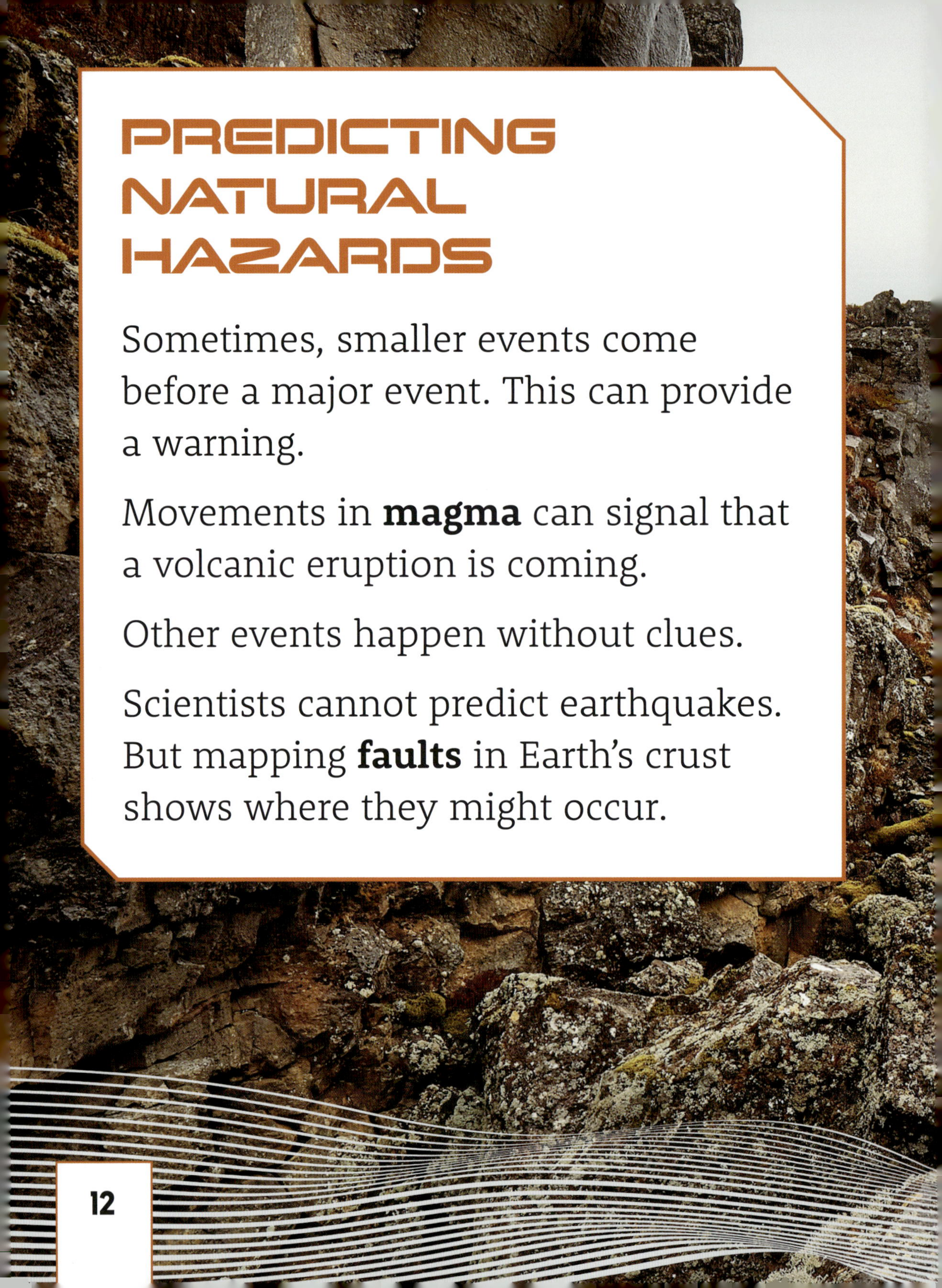

PREDICTING NATURAL HAZARDS

Sometimes, smaller events come before a major event. This can provide a warning.

Movements in **magma** can signal that a volcanic eruption is coming.

Other events happen without clues.

Scientists cannot predict earthquakes. But mapping **faults** in Earth's crust shows where they might occur.

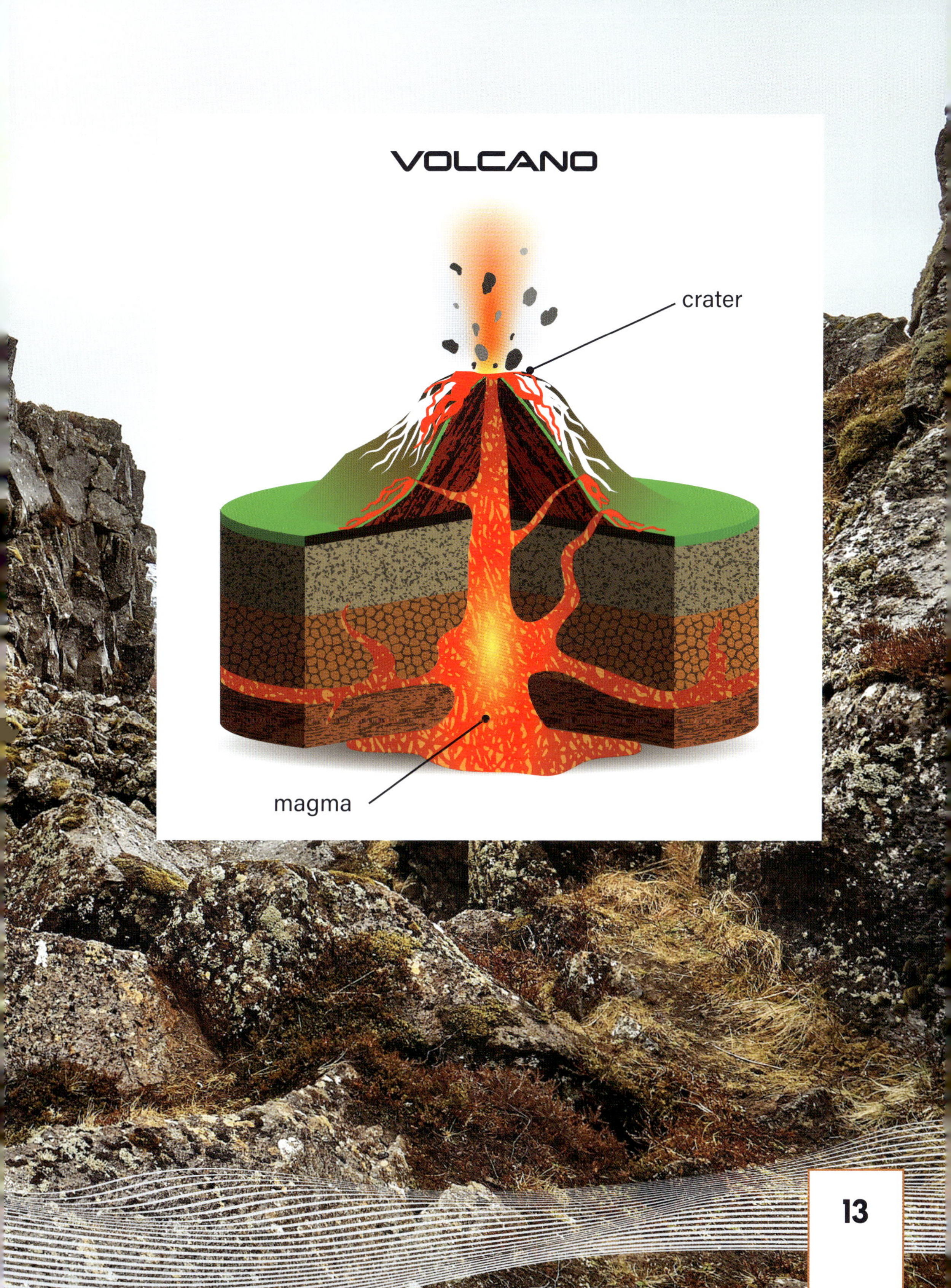
VOLCANO
crater
magma

PREPARING FOR NATURAL HAZARDS

Natural hazards cannot be eliminated. But people can take steps to reduce their impact.

In areas that have earthquakes, homes are built to withstand shaking ground.

Warning systems save lives by telling people to **evacuate** when there is a tsunami or a hurricane on the way.

People buy extra food, water, and sources of power to get ready for storms.

FUN FACTS

After Hurricane Andrew in 1992, the South Florida Building Code required stronger roofs, impact-resistant windows, and hurricane shutters on new buildings.

RECOVERING FROM NATURAL DISASTERS

When natural hazards become natural disasters, help is needed.

Some families need temporary housing if their homes are damaged or destroyed.

Organizations like the Red Cross give food and clothing to those in need.

Communities come together to help rebuild.

American
Red Cross
Disaster Relief
E 6 St
AMBULANCE

CAREER: HURRICANE HUNTER

A hurricane hunter's mission is to travel on planes directly through hurricanes and other storms. This lets them gather data about weather events.

Their specially designed jets fly high and fast.

Some hurricane hunters work for the National Oceanic and Atmospheric Administration (NOAA).

Others are part of the United States Air Force Reserve's 53rd Weather Reconnaissance Squadron.

INVESTIGATE: STORM SURGE

Materials:

- Small, shallow aluminum cake pan
- Play-Doh or clay
- Toy houses, cars, trees, etc.
- Sand
- Water
- Hair dryer or small fan
- Gravel, pebbles, or stones (optional)

Procedure:

(1) Press a layer of Play-Doh or clay onto one half of the cake pan to represent land. Make sure it goes to the edges of the pan. Use the toy houses, cars, trees, and other items to create a village on the land.

(2) Spread the other side of the pan with a layer of sand to represent the ocean floor. Make sure that it touches the land.

(3) Carefully pour water onto the ocean floor. Make sure the water does not go onto the land.

(4) Line up the hair dryer or fan so that it will blow across the water toward the land. Turn it on for 10 to 20 seconds to simulate the wind from a hurricane. Observe the effects of the storm surge.

Optional Activity:

(1) Add gravel, pebbles, or stones where the land and ocean meet.

(2) If needed, fix the village. Pour more water in the ocean.

(3) Use the hair dryer or fan to simulate more hurricane-force winds. Observe any changes. Make a conclusion.

THE SCIENTIFIC METHOD

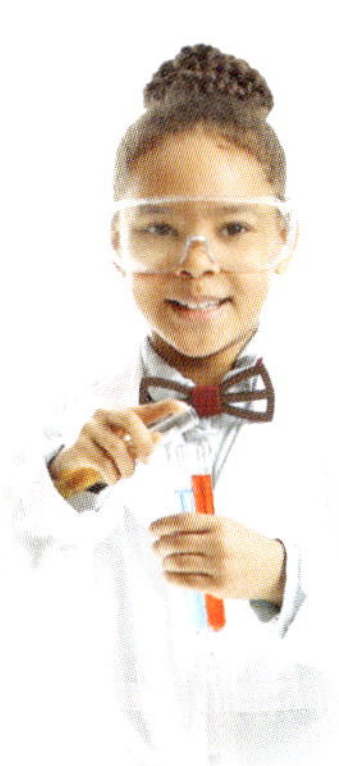

- Ask a question.
- Gather information and observe.
- Make a hypothesis or guess the answer.
- Experiment and test your hypothesis, or guess.
- Analyze your test results.
- Modify your hypothesis, if necessary.
- Make a conclusion.

SCIENTIST SPOTLIGHT

Edouard Benedictus was a French chemist, artist, and inventor. One day, he accidentally knocked a glass flask off a shelf. However, the pieces of broken glass held together. This was because a liquid plastic had dried and left a thin film on the inside of the flask. Benedictus used this idea to create safety glass for car windshields. Today, safety glass is also used for impact-resistant windows in areas with hurricanes.

GLOSSARY

atmosphere (AT-muhs-feer): the mixture of gases that surrounds a planet; all the air between the surface of a planet and outer space

disaster (di-ZAS-tur): an event that causes great damage or loss of life

droughts (drouts): periods of abnormally dry weather; long times without rain

earthquakes (URTH-kwayks): periods of sudden, violent shaking of the ground caused by movement in the tectonic plates that make up Earth's crust

evacuate (i-VAK-yoo-ate): to move from a dangerous place to somewhere safer

faults (fawlts): cracks in Earth's crust where tectonic plates rub against each other and where earthquakes are likely to occur

hazard (HAZ-urd): a chance of danger

hurricane (HUR-i-kane): a tropical storm with winds at a constant speed of at least 74 miles (119 kilometers) per hour

magma (MAG-muh): molten and semi-molten rock below Earth's surface that becomes lava when it flows out of volcanoes; magma makes up the layer of Earth called the mantle

tsunamis (tsu-NAH-mees): huge, destructive ocean waves caused by underwater earthquakes or volcanoes

AFTER READING QUESTIONS

1. What is the difference between a natural hazard and a natural disaster?

2. What are some types of natural hazards?

3. Why do you think it is important to know about natural hazards?

ABOUT THE AUTHOR

Christina Earley lives in South Florida with her husband, son, and dog. Her favorite subject in school was science. She enjoys learning the science behind the world around her, such as how roller coasters work. She loves mint chocolate chip ice cream and mermaids.

Written by: Christina Earley
Design by: Kathy Walsh
Editor: Kim Thompson

Photographs/Shutterstock: Cover & Title pg: Toa55, Benny Marty, Aksenova Nadezhd, amudsenh; p 4-23: amudsenh; p 5, 9, 11, 15: Hildskjalf; p 4 TlgoZh; p 5: Designua; p 6: Lucky Team Studio; p 7: 4.murat, Wead; p 8: LouiesWorld1; p 9: @Wiki; p 10: Filip Kosnik; p 11: Petro Perutskyi, aappp; p 12: Peter Gudella; p 13: Ellen Bronstayn; p 14: Tad Denson; p 15: Darwin Brandis; p 16: MDay Photography; p 17: a katz; p 18: Guido Amrein Switzerland; p 19: Jessica L. Kendziorek, U.S. AIR FORCE, Alex Erwin; p 21: Roman Zaiets, Pixel-Shot

Library of Congress PCN Data
Natural Hazards / Christina Earley
Earth and Space Science
ISBN 979-8-8873-5363-0 (hard cover)
ISBN 979-8-8873-5448-4 (paperback)
ISBN 979-8-8873-5533-7 (EPUB)
ISBN 979-8-8873-5618-1 (eBook)
Library of Congress Control Number: 2023930206

Printed in the United States of America.

Seahorse Publishing Company
www.seahorsepub.com

Published in the United States
Seahorse Publishing
PO Box 771325
Coral Springs, FL 33077